Amazing
AEROPLANES

For Jan and Billy – T.M.
For Henry and Horace – A.P.

The Publisher thanks the British Airways Community Learning Centre at
Heathrow Airport in London for their kind assistance in the development of this book.

First published by Kingfisher 2002
This edition published 2013 by Macmillan Children's Books
an imprint of Pan Macmillan, a division of
Macmillan Publishers International Limited
20 New Wharf Road, London N1 9RR
Associated companies throughout the world
www.panmacmillan.com

ISBN: 978-1-4472-1260-7

Text copyright © Tony Mitton 2002
Illustrations copyright © Ant Parker 2002
Moral rights asserted.

5 7 9 8 6

A CIP catalogue record for this book
is available from the British Library.

Printed in China

Amazing
AEROPLANES

Tony Mitton and
Ant Parker

MACMILLAN CHILDREN'S BOOKS

Whoosh

An aeroplane's amazing,
for it travels through the sky,

above the clouds, for miles and miles,
so very fast and high!

An airport is the place you go
to take a trip by air.

You check in at the terminal to show
you've paid your fare.

The ground crew weigh your baggage
and load it in the hold.

And then you take the walkway to the plane,
when you are told.

The flight deck's where the captain
and co-pilot do their jobs.
They both know how to fly the plane
with all its dials and knobs.

They radio Control Tower to check
the runway's clear.
They can't take off unless it is,
with other planes so near.

By intercom, the captain on the flight deck says hello.

You have to do your seat belt up,
before the plane can go!

A plane is big and heavy,
yet it climbs up really high.

It zooms along the runway
and soars into the sky.

Its wings hold big jet engines,
which are loud and very strong.
They suck in air and blow it through
to whoosh the plane along.

When the plane moves fast enough,
the air around's so swift
it pushes up beneath the wings
and makes the whole plane lift.

Soon the plane is in the air,
so now you're on your flight.
The cabin crew look after you
and see that you're all right.

They bring you drinks and magazines
and trays of food to eat.
And sometimes there's a film to watch
while sitting in your seat.

When the journey's over,
the captain lands the plane.
Control Tower have to say it's safe
for coming down again.

You sit with seat belt fastened,
there's a bumpy, rumbling sound –
the wheels are making contact
and the plane is on the ground!

At last the doors are opening.
Then out you come with smiles.

So give a cheer! For look, you're here.
You've flown for miles and miles.

Aeroplane bits

control tower
from here the air traffic controllers direct the planes and tell pilots when to take off and land safely

flight deck
sometimes called the **cockpit** this is where the pilot and co-pilot sit

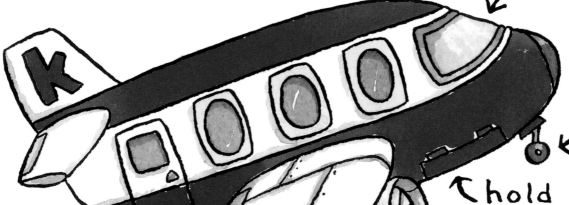

wheel
the wheels fold away while the plane is in the air

hold
this is the space where heavy luggage is stored

wing →
the wings are hollow to make them as light as possible and a smooth shape so they move through the air easily

jet engine
jet engines blow out air and gas to push the plane forward – the gas is made by burning fuel

terminal
this is the building at the airport where passengers go to catch a plane

TERMINAL